Just Passing Through

Poems by Mick Blackistone
Photographs by Marion E. Warren

Schiffer Publishing Ltd®

4880 Lower Valley Road   Atglen, Pennsylvania   19310
Printed in China

We walked
many a crooked path
you and me
never could get things straight
                    could we

and
even now
when we thought
they'd never find us
our hide-a-way
at the end of another
            crooked path
we hear the sound
of the bulldozers
                    still

daydreaming
    of blue sky
    and
    open water
uncluttered and free
to seek my bounty
    lying beyond
      beneath
the abyss
    patiently waiting
with teasing illusions
knowing
    I can't stay away
      too long

you remind me of a fresh spring morning
bathed in sunlight
                and the smell of newborn violets

you remind me of a snowy evening
fresh with life dressed in a white blouse
                gleaming in a moonbeam

you remind me of a misty sea
calm under a shroud of enthusiasm
        waiting to break loose and carry me away

you remind me of life
              so often
that my excitement is overwhelming

finally, you remind me of love and peace
              happiness and warmth
because I receive so much from you
                  Miss Edith

who knows
what's real anymore
as we step
                    between
delusion and illusion
our hearts
our minds
our souls
on display
as we try
          to close ourselves off
from
          what's real
                         anymore

in the throws
of confusion
    frustration
    apprehension
    isolation
    rebellion
my energy burned
            seeking
freedom in flight
there was hope out there
      somewhere anywhere
and then
      quite simply
my search ended
           with you

footsteps tread through the mountain
draped with the mellowing of dawn
silent
    sliding
        footsteps mark the passage
        to where I will meet you
the mountain is beautiful here
sounds are silent
                    beneath the power
of the granite rumbling impatiently
in anticipation
          of our meeting
          in its shadow veil
to feel the emotion
              of nature's naked passion

through it all,
you were there
 when I need you
 the most
when
 my vision blurred
and
 my voice cracked
you were there
when
 my strength failed
and
 my heart ached
you were there
surrounded
by familiar strangers
I knew
 I could always
lean on you

Somehow
we put our lives together,
piece by piece, bit by bit
And we had to tweak it now and again
to get it just right

Somehow
we put our lives together
with a little of this and a little of that
We had to bend the rules
to get it just right

Somehow
we put our lives together
and I'm glad we figured it out

"What's the matter with you?" she demanded.
"Make something of yourself!"
"When are you going to straighten up?"

Echoing through
the caverns of my mind,
she
    haunts me still
as I
    lie beneath the covers in a fetal position,
thinking
    about where I'll be
             tomorrow

Probably hauling oysters
             from that old river
saying to Miss Katherine's ghost:

"I may straighten up
       one day."

sometimes

        it's good to be home

with friends

and familiar surroundings

back

to what is sacred

where

      the water's voice

is that of your father's

where

      the sand's warmth

is that of your mother's

and the blood

in your veins

        flows through

to your brothers

Sunday
we gather together
as we always have
brothers
    in communion
    offering confession
cleansing our spirits
by
  swapping lies
  telling tales
  bluffing our way through
          another Sunday

So many men have passed this way,
remembering your name
and the memories
                good and bad
long nights
        spent with you
        in quiet company
as you carried their dreams
from here to there
            and back again
you listened
        to their fears
        and tears
        and laughter
you knew all their secrets
and then
    they would leave
after
   spending time with you
   trusting you
        would deliver
        all they expected
and you
    never let them down

time was
    when they ran
    between your shadows
    amidst
        tears and laughter
    which
crowded storefronts
between rows of vegetables
                    seed
                    tools
                    fabrics which wove
them all together
and lifted their spirits
                in paradise
time was
    when they looked
    beyond the edge of town
    to seek
        far-reaching heights
and
    left you
        behind

It's hard for me
            to know sometimes
where your thoughts are
because
so often
we are in different places
            at different times
I speculate
            then hesitate
and decide to wait
for you to reach me
because you know
                I'm here
                    for you

"Why should I stay?" I asked.
"The answer is here," he said.

"Listen to the silence
broken by
 the muskrat working the grass
 the songs of the cricket
  croak of the frog
  purr of the diesel.
"Reach out and embrace the breeze
  the dawn's dampness
  the weathered wood.
Lift your head and smell the marsh
  the saltwater
  remnants of fish and crab.
"Open your eyes and see the wonders
  never always changing."

"The answer is here," I said.
"Why would you want to leave?" he asked.

I don't know
about the names of things
or
what makes
        this old world turn
I don't know
about the what and why
or
when people
        chose to walk alone
I don't know
about life or death
or
where you
        might fit in

All I know
is my own heart
when
    I think from time to time
and that I may be here
tomorrow
if you're just passing by
whether
        king or vagabond

Like statues
          they were there
from first to last
                    light
and through each new moon
          they were there
silently
          watching
                    waiting
as the world ran by

How long can
that old porch
                    stand the strain?

after all
  is said and done
and the great
   philosophers
dissect the intricacies
of the season ... our season
      ... our ins and outs
      ... our depth of commitment
      ... our resistance to change
we can look them
    straight in the eye
and say
  quite eloquently,
hell, we know enough
    to get by

Quietly nestled
among friends
            I contemplate
your existence
covered
in a cloak of white
facing another dawn
you remain idle

Where is the winter rapture,
the banging
      loading
      talking
      laughing?
Where are the men
who make footprints
                  on your soul
covered in a cloak of rubber and wool

Probably
      nestled quietly
among friends
            contemplating
their existence

rest
	weary in your solitude
knowing
that deep within the marrow
of your soul
lay
the memories of transients
generations
			passed by
you carried their secrets
and
	honor them still
deep within the marrow
			of your soul

What lies beyond
the bend
     in the road
I don't know

What waits for you
round there
I don't know

What stands here
is all
    I know
but I can walk
       this far
         with you

Evening
       we are alone now
yellow piercing brown
silky shadows slowly shimmering
               alone
... listening
      ... watching
          ... waiting
Mother nature
surrounds us
with her shadow soldiers
I'm glad you are with me
            alone
... listening
      ... watching
          ... waiting
for what
the shadows
       come closer now
the cove responds
      to embrace
welcome us
and it's good
      to be among friends
         alone

We spend time
searching
          throughout tomorrow
to find secluded answers
deep within the shadows
                    of our minds

We are content in our search
for it is done together
                    as one
as it should be
          as we will be
                    as we are
and it is good to be together
no. . .
we are not lost
for we are together
in a search to find a way
                    there is a way
we know there is a way
together
          so that what we are searching for
we can eventually say
                    we found yesterday
                              together . . .

If we pause
    will you share
    your wisdom
with us
    as you rest
    your weary mind

If we stop
    will you share
    your thoughts
with us
    so we know
    about the unknown

If we sit
    will you share
    your wealth
with us
    less fortunate
    with little to give
besides
    there's an empty chair
    and we need to be near
            you

I awoke last night
          around midnight
to eavesdrop on your conversation
you were caught up
          in your own circumstances
and gave
          little consideration
          to my presence
perhaps
          at midnight
I was of little consequence
in the scheme of things
          tonight
          you will be gone
and I
   will be left
          alone
to recall the conversation
and hope
          for a chance
          to eavesdrop
              again

They played
                the game for years
Then one day
                everything was right
to make a move
and
        we watched, waited
        in anticipation
        anxious
in our own
                anxiety as
this old slowpoke
swallowed his pride
prepared to make a move
on a
        foxy lady
and
we never knew
who came out ahead
neither do they
                but
they're still playing the game
                                today

I've been thinking lately.
Maybe we should make some changes.
Nothing dramatic you understand.
But, I suppose,
      we could do a few things
to make our relationship
a little,
      just a little,
            more exciting.
I treasure my time with you.
The open relationship,
      times of silent reflection,
            planning.
Even when I'm furious with you
I'd rather still be with you
      than somewhere else.
Yea, we should make some changes.
I think they'd make us feel better
even though we feel good now.
Just something small to start with.
So,
   anyway,
      I'll get the paint.

who said
        we couldn't do it
        you and I,
as we stood
                in the emptiness
waiting for something
                to lift
        our spirits
and
who said
        we wouldn't make a difference
        you and I
as we took the dare
        through the fear
        between apprehension and
                                self doubt
stepping forward
                to try

hope
moved desperately
taking
    the hand of **faith**
which lingered slowly
stood stoically
with **patience**
         and together
all three helped
push you
closer to your dream

barefoot they ran
    the dreamers and believers
    the schemers and deceivers
the mothers
          of the mothers'
             children
escaping to you
running from you
trying
    to find their way
and you
    remain
forgotten
but
    for them still

Hey,
what are you going to do about it?
Remain asleep
      apathetic
      or run some more?
I didn't ask to deserve this
I don't want your sympathy
          compassion
          understanding
Just an answer to my question,
what are you going to do about it anyway?
I need to know
so I can face tomorrow.
Please.

The sun slips by
and memories
buried beneath furrowed brow
separate
      wheat from chaf
letting me explore
peacefully
the simple
    elegant
        treasures
of my day

This spot
        the here and now
gives us hope
that there can be something
eternal
        left unchanged
by selfish desires
and that
        over time
it will remain
for us
when we return

I suppose
there could be a prettier spot
                                somewhere...
but
I can't place it right now

what's it to you
            where I go
who hurts me
            secrets I know
the depths of perception
the heights of frustration
I may not
            go anywhere
I may remain
            to myself right here
and hope
            you'll care for me one day

They said
        you were gone
to
more exotic places
Bullshit
        I said
Have some faith
and then
when
I turned around
you were there
when
    I needed you
            the most

your face
        marks the passage of time
as you follow your mind's eye
to search
        through ancient visions
and
your face
        traces many passages
        with hope
        and
        optimism that there will be
a time and passage
        for your tomorrow

The sun
      beat down for centuries
burning through the morning.
They thought
        you could ignore it
        and the pain
as you
      pulled, prodded, picked
through
      your options
trying to cope
with what your heart
          desired.

How long
      have you been out here anyway?
      out of the way?

Friends go to the country
       to rest and escape
       to get away from it all
       leave problems behind
go
   where time doesn't change much
   and values remain the same
   from generation to generation
most stay only a short time
it's refreshing, they say
some stay longer
       become part of the cycle
       from generation to generation
       and they are better for it I suppose

they say
I might not be able
to work this out
    that the times are tough
    that I'm too old
    that the market's soft
    and the weather's bad
I told them
I've been here
long before
    they thought of arriving
    and
    the farm was here
    long before me
I told them
not to worry about
my hard times
and that I'd be happy
to stay on as caretaker
of the land
because it's brought me
this far and
without their help
thank you

We could do something about it I suppose
that is
    if we knew what it is
    we would do something about
and then again
    once we figured it out
we might just decide
    to sit here some more
and discuss our options

So. . . What do you think?
I don't.

So. . . What do you feel?
I don't.

So. . . What do you know?
I don't.

So. . . What do you say?
I don't.

So. . . What can I do for you?
Leave me to wait for my friend.

know what?
     no one will know
what went on here
since we've come
     to this place...
left our mark
lit a spark
did our best
like the rest
who came to this place before us...
it's okay
     we know
what went on here and
in the morning
     we'll be gone...

A long time ago
we decided to stay
you and me
stick it out
fighting
      solitude
      drought
      insects
      foreclosure
we could barely stand
      the excitement
and here we are
you and me

it's still exciting
to be with you

I don't know
            things are just different here
it's quiet
        time waits for you
you may catch up
            you may not
I know what it's like over there
I lived there
remember
anyway
        for now
I will live here
while
you survive there
                and it's been nice
                talking to you over there

Sometimes
when I contemplate
my existence
        where I am
        could have been
my mind
   reaches for your touch
and
   your body
        in my hands
responds
     slowly
        embracing my fingers
and
   I know
     I am happiest
        with you

We have to say good-bye
today
to generations
    of joy and tears
    of forgotten dreams
    of fading memories
    of future plans
it's been a long time
coming
but we're here now
to watch the crowd
wave good-bye

look

we can't keep fooling around like this

me chasing you

               you avoiding me

we've been carrying on

for too long

and it's time

we got down to terms

with destiny

perhaps it was fate

               that brought us together

I don't know

but

now it's time

               to move toward

                     the kitchen

Worry not of yesterday:

          It has been lost in the shadows.

Worry not of tomorrow:

          It will be found in the sun.

Worry not of today:

          It is our celebration for being together.

There's a place
        to search
            seek
            solitude
        to find or lose
whichever
choose
up there or down here
anywhere
        to escape or return
        to what your heart remembers

how long
have you been sitting here
    waiting
    reaching
for your life's quota
    silently
    swiftly
nimble gnarled fingers
constantly moving
and
the songs of generations
break the boredom
set the rhythm
remove you from here
    to there
    and back tomorrow

Oh Chesapeake
     you mythical mistress
     protecting your children
who come calling and crying
helpless without your embrace
accept me as a stranger
in your midst
I promise
I won't be here long

Going through the motions
                    secrets
                    caressing each moment
                    questioning each feeling
tasting the sweat
feeling the pain
                    as muscles tighten
                    withdraw
anticipating completion
                    of your creation
you can give birth
                    with a smile
knowing the ritual
                    will be repeated again

one day when the world
isn't watching
I will once again
    crawl up on you
    and lie within your embrace
as you gently sway
to the rhythm
    of the sea
    and moan to the motions
    of all that is created
within your soul

                kathy lynn

you always ran from me
into the shroud of your own existence
and even now
as I hold your body
you want to escape again
to the shadows of your own
misgivings
until the next time
when I reach for you
and embrace you with
my own

we watched
as you stood sentry,
silently
beside the shadows
of an aging fortress
and
we knew nothing
could sneak by you

If you like prospectin'
and
diggin' in the mud
then
I might have a spot
for you
with no guarantees
but
    a full meal
    a sore back
    a dirty hat
    a tall tale
and a ride back to shore

I didn't come here
looking for much
'bout all I wanted
was
    a clean shirt
    and
    a nice boat
but
I didn't find either one
despite the disappointment
I'm glad I stayed anyway

no
we don't have neon lights
or
neon ladies
fact
we don't have gourmet coffee
or
gourmet kitchens
but
we have a nice peeler run
in the spring
and
a nice soft crab sandwich
and besides
this is as good a place as any
to hang my hat

I asked him
why do you like it out here?
He said it reached into
    the marrow of his soul
and
    pulled him to the essence of life
He said it allowed him to pierce the silence
    with a click of the shutter
    to capture the spirit
of the quest for me

Ain't much to do I suppose
except to wait for the weather
to lay down for awhile

Ain't much to say I suppose
except to wonder about fate
and what's in store
for us tomorrow

sometimes in the throws of searching
I wonder what's the point
of looking for you
you always were evasive
despite my persistence
and yet I knew
at one magic moment
you would be there

She said to follow the road,
that I had to choose
    between winning and losing
    between the straight and the narrow
    between searching and gambling

She said to look into my mind,
to see that I could choose
    between winning and losing
    between the light and the dark

What's the use?
I keep thinking the same thing.
Well, we keep trying
and we keep asking, what's the use?
and we keep doing the same thing
day in and day out
but one day
I'm going to quit holding up
this ol' piling.

Other Schiffer Books by the Author:
Dancing with the Tide: Watermen of the Chesapeake, 978-0-8703-3532-7, $24.95
Broken Wings Will Fly, 978-0-8703-3439-9, $10.95

Other Schiffer Books on Related Subjects:
The Watermen of the Chesapeake Bay, 978-0-8703-3374-3, $34.95
Bodine's Chesapeake Bay Country, 978-0-8703-3562-4, $29.95

Type set in New Baskerville
ISBN: 978-0-7643-3991-2
Printed in China

Schiffer Books are available at special discounts for bulk purchases for sales promotions or premiums. Special editions, including personalized covers, corporate imprints, and excerpts can be created in large quantities for special needs. For more information contact the publisher:

Published by Schiffer Publishing Ltd.
4880 Lower Valley Road
Atglen, PA 19310
Phone: (610) 593-1777; Fax: (610) 593-2002
E-mail: Info@schifferbooks.com

For the largest selection of fine reference books on this and related subjects, please visit our website at:
www.schifferbooks.com
We are always looking for people to write books on new and related subjects. If you have an idea for a book, please contact us at
proposals@schifferbooks.com

This book may be purchased from the publisher.
Include $5.00 for shipping.
Please try your bookstore first.
You may write for a free catalog.

In Europe, Schiffer books are distributed by
Bushwood Books
6 Marksbury Ave.
Kew Gardens
Surrey TW9 4JF England
Phone: 44 (0) 20 8392 8585; Fax: 44 (0) 20 8392 9876
E-mail: info@bushwoodbooks.co.uk
Website: www.bushwoodbooks.co.uk